Toolkit #8

Gift Acceptance Policies

Why your nonprofit needs them
and how to develop

Marilyn L. Donnellan, MS

Gift Acceptance Policies
Why your nonprofit needs them and how to develop

ISBN 9798639494086

Nonprofit Toolkits:

Toolkit #1: Volunteer Handbooks

Toolkit #2: The Top Twenty Sustainability Strategies for Nonprofits

Toolkit #3: Becoming a Tech-Focused Nonprofit

Toolkit #4: ED Succession Plans and Search Process

Toolkit #5: Developing and Marketing a Story-Telling Budget

Toolkit #6: 10 Key Strategies for Responding to Disasters

Toolkit #7: Communication & Conflict

Toolkit #8: Gift Acceptance Policies

Published by Kindle Direct Publishing
©2020, by Marilyn L. Donnellan, MS, Author

Table of Contents

Introduction

I was a brand-new executive director at a one-staff (me) nonprofit when I had my first experience with controversial donations. Still wet behind the ears, I excitedly accepted our first tangible gift: a dozen compact printers. I was charged by our national association to disburse the printers to nonprofits in our community.

A few weeks after the donation, I walked into the office of one of the recipient nonprofits and was shocked to see the printer being used as a doorstop.

When I asked the executive director (ED) about it, he replied, "It is useless. It won't print worth a darn and the ink cartridges are too expensive."

I contacted the association to find out what was going on. We had paid the shipping costs, an expense we could barely afford.

"XYZ company is one of our largest contributors. They asked us to accept the donation to allow them to write the printers off as a tax deduction. We did not know they didn't work."

The association fell into the same donation trap many of us in nonprofits inadvertently do. In our attempt to make the donor happy and gain needed resources for our nonprofits, we get ourselves into untenable situations. We accept donations (cash or tangible items) which do not fit with our mission, are too expensive to dispose of or are from donors whose values are totally opposite of ours.

How can we prevent that from happening?

Chapter One
Purpose of Gift Acceptance Policies

Gift acceptance policies can provide guidelines to your nonprofit and donors. Such policies will go a long ways toward preventing problems for both.

Consider what would happen if your nonprofit, with a focus on environmental issues, was offered a $500,000 cash gift by a large oil company, a company you were suing for unsafe emissions. The gift could be a huge boost to the nonprofit's ability to fulfill the mission.

If you as a far-sighted ED guided the nonprofit in the development of a comprehensive gift acceptance policy a few years earlier, it would make the decision easier.

The nonprofit would undoubtedly decide the mission was more important than the money, based on your board-approved policies. You would graciously thank the donor, give them a copy of the gift acceptance policies, and say, "Thanks, but no thanks."

In this hypothetical situation, accepting the donation had two perils associated with it:

1. Conflict of interest – Because the donor was being sued by the nonprofit, the gift could be viewed as a bribe to stop the lawsuit.
2. Conflict with the mission – The donor's business clearly violated the mission and values of the nonprofit.

When done right, gift acceptance policies provide guidance to you and the board of directors, staff, and donors on acceptable and unacceptable gifts.

In the example of the environmental nonprofit, the policies approved by the board and reviewed by their attorney, would keep them out of legal trouble, and easily expedite and depersonalize the denial process.

These types of gift policies are a requirement for nonprofits, as listed on the Internal Revenue Service (IRS) 990 form, filed annually by all nonprofits. Few of the hundreds of nonprofits I have worked with as a consultant have such policies. Many put a checkmark in the IRS 990 form, indicating they have gift acceptance policies, but few have more than a one or two sentence statement or it is in the ED's head, not on paper.

Best practices for nonprofits indicate a need for these policies to protect your organization from accepting controversial donations, or tangible items which are too expensive or unwieldy to manage.

Naïve resource development staff, in their eagerness to please donors, can inadvertently put the organization into financial and ethical dilemmas when there are no policies to guide them.

A small church was given $10 million from the lottery winnings of a parishioner. Although the pastor of the church regularly preached against gambling, it was apparently too much money to pass up. Ten years after squandering the money on a huge, elaborate facility with three swimming pools and two worship centers, the church went bankrupt. There was no one on staff qualified to administer such large amounts of money or to develop plans for long-term sustainability. Their greed overcame their good sense.

There are nine specific reasons why gift acceptance policies are essential for your nonprofit:

1. To manage expectations of donors
2. Provides guidelines for the board and staff
3. Ensures adherence to nonprofit values and mission
4. Avoids legal implications
5. Limits disposal issues of unwanted tangible items
6. Meets standards and best practices for nonprofits
7. Adheres to IRS 990 requirements
8. Expedites acceptance or denial process
9. Depersonalizes decision making.

Before you develop the gift acceptance policies, be sure everyone involved understands the reasons for the policies. Briefly outline the rationale for the policies at the beginning of the policy manual.

There are two types of gift acceptance policies:

- An individual donor or a company's document outlining their parameters for making donations of goods, services, or cash
- A set of policies developed by a donation committee and presented to the nonprofit board of directors for approval. Procedures for implementation are developed by the ED.

Chapter Two
Define Terms

As you start developing gift acceptance policies, define terms you will be using in the policies. Like any effective communication strategy, starting with definitions will clarify meanings and reduce conflicts. Typical definitions of relevant terms are listed below in alphabetical order:

Brand Identity
The vision or personality of the organization. Brand identities can be good or bad, depending on your nonprofit's reputation.

Coercion
The practice by some organizations or businesses to try to force individual donations (e.g. workplace fundraising campaigns) in order to improve their standing in the community or to increase donations.

Controversial Donations
The donations of any organization or individual whose ethics and values do not match those of the recipient nonprofit.

Donate a Gift or "Donation"
In its simplest terms, donating a gift is defined as the transfer of title or possession of something from a person or entity to a nonprofit with no expectation

or consideration of payment. This includes cash and tangible items.

Donation Committee

A designated group of volunteers and staff who evaluate controversial or unusual donations of cash or tangible items and determine the gifts compliance with your organization's gift acceptance policies. This committee might also be responsible for the development of the initial policies to go to the board of directors for approval, and then reviewing them at least annually to make sure they are still relevant.

Donor Bill of Rights

A document outlining a donor's tangible and intangible rights (Addendum A), used to inform donors and potential donors and to protect their rights to privacy and information.

Ethics and Values

Moral principles which guide your nonprofit's decision making are defined as "ethics," while "values" are defined as principles or standards of behavior.

Codes of conduct are based on ethics, while values are based on your nonprofit's sense of right and wrong behavior. Although the terms are often used interchangeably, they are different. If your organization has a controversial mission, clear definitions of ethics and values will drive any gift acceptance policies.

Fair Market Value or Valuation

For a donor to receive a tax deduction on a donation of a tangible item, and for your nonprofit to record the value, the donor and the organization agree on the fair market value or price.

If, for example, a house or property was donated, the formula to determine fair market is based on gathering prices on three comparable properties, adding the prices, and dividing by three (e.g. total of $330,000 divided by three, equals $110,000). In this illustration, fair market value is $110,00 with a range of a low price of $100,000 and a high price of $120,000.

Gifts in Kind

Goods and services donated instead of cash are referred to as "gifts in kind."

Named Gifts

Any donations which will result in a property, building or other tangible item named on behalf of the donor.

Non-standard Contributions

IRS defines non-standard contributions as any "item that is not reasonably expected to be used to satisfy or further your nonprofit's exempt purposes and for which:

    a) There is no ready market to liquidate the donation to convert it to cash, and

    b) The value of the item is difficult to ascertain or speculate."

Philanthropy

The promotion of the welfare of others and organizations serving their needs, by the donation of goods, services, or cash.

Planned Giving

A planned gift is a donation arranged for allocation at a future date (such as upon the donor's death). Wills, charitable remainder trusts and other instruments are generally used to express the donor's wishes.

Pre-arranged Sale

A charitable gift can be denied, or the tax benefits overturned by IRS, if the donor has proceeded too far in selling the property before contributing it to a nonprofit, known as a "pre-arranged sale."

Related Use Gift

When your nonprofit uses a donated gift (such as property) in a manner consistent with its exempt, or related purpose it is referred to as a "related use gift." This is the opposite of "non-standard gifts."

Tax-Deductible Organizations

Defined by IRS 501(c) code as a tax-exempt organization (such as 501(c)3 organizations) which is eligible for donations by individuals, businesses or corporations and are tax-deductible for the donor, according to IRS tax laws.

Tax-Exempt Organizations

Defined by IRS 501 code as a nonprofit organization organized for public benefit which is eligible to not pay taxes. Certain tax-exempt categories (such as a 501(c)6 organization) are NOT tax-deductible by the donor.

Unrelated Business Income Tax (UBI)

According to the IRS code, UBI refers to any activity to generate income which is not related to the tax-exempt purposes of the nonprofit. Such activities, services or donations could be subject to UBI taxes.

Chapter Three
Establish Guidelines for Policies

There are specific guidelines to consider before drafting your gift acceptance policies. Some of these guidelines are related to the nonprofit and some to the donor. The guidelines are arranged in three categories: donors, nonprofits, and the gift. The guidelines are based on best practices as determined by national or international standards developed by experienced nonprofits and nonprofit professionals.

Donor Guidelines

The Donor Bill of Rights (Addendum A) is a great place to start in developing guidelines for donors. When developing this type of document, put yourself in the donor's place and think about the things important to you as a donor to your favorite charity.

Additional issues to consider including in the Bill of Rights include:

- The importance of contacting the donor's tax advisor
- Confidentiality of donations, unless the donor is willing to accept public recognition
- How donors will be recognized
- The right to not be coerced to donate.

Nonprofit Guidelines

The sample policies in Addendum B cover most of the issues the nonprofit needs to consider in developing their gift acceptance policies, as well as some simple policies to get you started. Typical policies to include are related to the following:

- When legal counsel will be sought
- A statement that your nonprofit cannot give tax advice
- How the gift acceptance committee will be developed and their duties (job description)
- Ethics, values, vision, and mission
- Forbidding coercion of any type.

The Gift Guidelines

While developing gift acceptance policies, the designated committee may recommend to the designated committee (like the Resource Development Committee - RD) that different levels of giving be established, such as leadership giving programs. Fig. 1 shows a typical board standing committee structure. Notice planned giving, gifts in kind and leadership giving are included as the RD committee's responsibilities. Add the gift acceptance responsibility to their tasks as a sub-committee's responsibilities to begin the process.

Include examples of appropriate and inappropriate gifts and the types of gifts accepted. Indication of the importance of all donations being consistent with the ethics, values and mission of the nonprofit is a critical policy.

Specify who in the organization is authorized to accept which types of gifts and the various levels of giving. The policy must clearly indicate any differences in recognition for cash and tangible items.

Gift policies should also include how tangible gifts, such as animals, stocks, property, jewelry life insurance, trusts, wills, etc., will be disposed of or used for income-producing strategies.

Fig. 1 – Board Standing Committee Structure

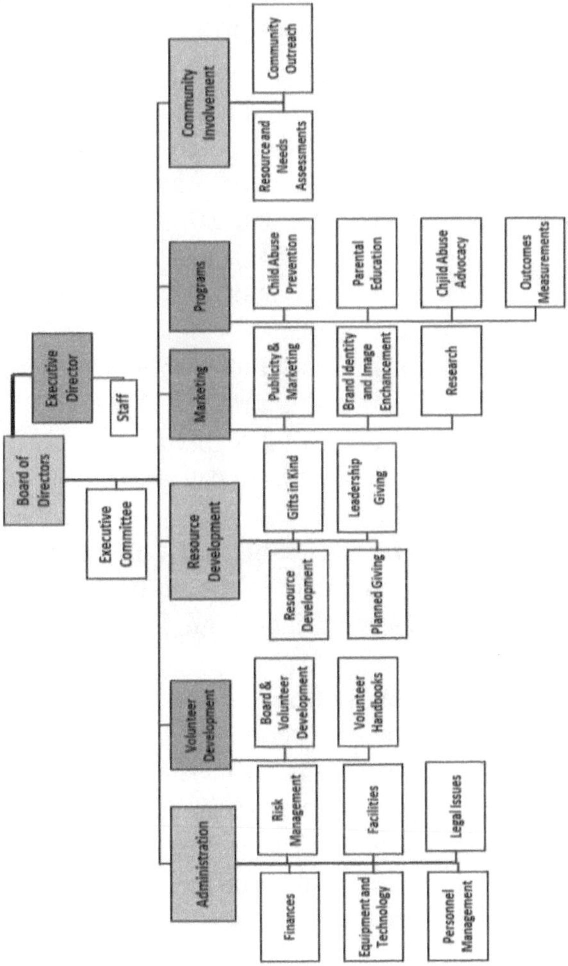

Chapter Four

Step #1: Determine Contents and Format of Gift Acceptance Policies and Procedures Manual

Developing the Gift Acceptance Policies (GAP) and procedures involves a series of steps. The first step is related to the Table of Contents. Putting together any type of policies and procedures manual is always easier if you first develop the draft table of contents. This will help to organize your thoughts around specific topics and what to include. You can always go back and narrow the topics or change them.

Although this sample table of contents is listed in the recommended order, feel free to revise it as you see fit. Your Gift Acceptance Manual (GAM) might include the following categories:

I.   Introduction and Table of Contents
Statement of the purpose of the manual and where sections are found (Addendum B)

II.   Definitions
Include terms used in the manual and their meanings, as shown in Chapter Two. Sometimes these definitions are included at the end of the manual, but I prefer them at the front in order to avoid confusion to the reader.

III. **Guidelines**

Specify the underlying rationale for the GAM, including relevant items listed in Chapter Two.

IV. **Mission, Vision, Ethics and Values' Statements**

By including these statements in the manual, you will show the basis for acceptance or denial of controversial gifts, and the foundation for all the policies and procedures.

V. **Donor Rights**

Based on the Donor Bill of Rights (Addendum A), the purpose of this section is to itemize the specific policies and procedures related to donors and potential donors.

VI. **Nonprofit Rights**

Statements related to the right of the nonprofit to accept or not accept a donation of tangible items or cash should be highlighted here.

VII. **Gift Acceptance Policies and Procedures**

Based on all the above issues, here is where specific policies and procedures are outlined, as in Addendum B.

It is recommended the format of the manual be computer based. This allows topics to be hyperlinked and used for searches of the document for specific issues. The policies can be part of the organization's policies and procedures manual or be separate from it. Either way, hyperlinks and searches are helpful.

The full manual could be available internally to all staff and volunteers, with a simplified and summarized version available on your website. Even more concise versions can be posted in the lobby of your organization and published in brochure format for potential donors.

I also prefer the use of tables for formatting the manual. Not only does this force you to be concise, but it makes for much easier reading, as shown at the beginning of Addendum C.

Chapter Five
Step #2 – Define the Philosophies Behind Gift Acceptance Policies

The basic philosophies of your organization will determine the gift acceptance policies. These philosophies are outlined in the vision, mission, ethics, and values of your nonprofit.

Vision and Mission

Many vision and mission statements are too long. These should be short, concise statements, reviewed at least every other year during the strategic planning updates. The statements should be no more than 25 words each.

The vision is **why** your nonprofit exists, the passion, brand identity and the primary goal to achieve, with no action verbs included. A child abuse prevention nonprofit might have as a vision: *"All children safe from abuse."*

Mission statements are **how** the vision is achieved (the programs) and include verbs. The same child abuse prevention nonprofit's mission could be: *"To educate the community, develop effective programs and support the victims of child abuse."*

Vision and mission statements are simple case statements and form the basis for more detailed case statements essential for all donor and grant appeals, as well as brand identity and marketing materials.

Whenever your donation committee, or RD, considers accepting a gift from a controversial organization or individual, the vision and mission statements provide the basic guidelines for decision making.

A child abuse prevention nonprofit would not accept a gift from an organization which supports the sexual abuse of children. There are such organizations, by the way. But the child abuse prevention nonprofit's vision and mission clearly state the reasons why such a gift would be unacceptable.

The book, [1]*Nonprofit Management Simplified: Board and Volunteer Development,* Chapter Two, provides step by step instructions on how to develop and evaluate good vision and mission statements.

Ethics Statements[2]

Although it is rare to find written ethics statements for nonprofits, they are foundational for guiding the actions of staff and volunteers. The often-unconscious, unstated ethics determine the right and wrong of any decision.

During the recent pandemic, health care workers were frequently confronted with ethical issues related to life or death, who lives and who dies.

The examples of ethics are based on a March 25, 2018 response to an online request of Jan Layton, a medical technologist.

- Integrity in personal and professional matters
- Honesty, truthfulness and sincerity

---

[1] ©2017, *Nonprofit Management Simplified: Board and Volunteer Development,* CharityChannel Press, by Marilyn L. Donnellan, MS, www.amazon.com/author/mldonnellan

[2] Jan Layton, Medical Technologist, FirstHealth Moore Regional Hospital

- Loyalty and allegiance
- Responsibility, reliability and dependability
- Charity and kindness
- Respect for others and their property
- Self-discipline and acting with reasonable restraint
- Knowing the distinction between right and wrong and good and bad behavior.

Developing these types of ethics statements is a great exercise for a board of directors or staff. Do not get caught up in wordsmithing or focusing so much on how things are worded that the essence of the statement is lost. Brainstorming is a great technique to use. The facilitator writes down on flip chart paper one or two-word responses to the questions, "What ethical statements drive our organization? What do we regard as right and wrong behavior?"

A designated group of two or three people could then take the results and put them into a list like the example above. The board of directors would review them and approve a final version.

Knowing what your organization's ethics are will help greatly in developing gift acceptance policies.

Values Statements

Ethics and values are often used interchangeably, but they are different. Ethics are the rules which govern the behavior of a group, organization or individual. Values are the beliefs which underpin the ethics.

Sometimes organizations will combine the two into "Ethics and Values Statements."

For individuals with an underlying religious belief, values are usually based on their primary religious texts, their founder, or their leader. Examples would be:

- Christians – The Bible (Old and New Testaments)
- Jews – The Torah
- Muslims – The Koran
- Mormons – The Book of Mormon

Values and ethics for the Christian and Jewish religions are based on the Ten Commandments:

1. No idolatry – "Thou shalt have no other gods before me."
2. No swearing – "Thou shalt not take the Name of the Lord thy God in vain."
3. Keep the Sabbath – "Thou shalt keep the Sabbath Day Holy."
4. Respect for elders – "Thou shalt honor thy father and mother."
5. No murder – "Thou shalt not kill."
6. No adultery – "Thou shalt not commit adultery."
7. Do not steal – "Thou shalt not steal."
8. Do not lie – "Thou shalt not bear false witness against thy neighbor."
9. Do not lust – "Do not let thyself lust after thy neighbor's wife."
10. Do not covet – "Thou shalt not covet thy neighbor's house, nor his farm, nor his cattle, nor anything that is his."

An organization wanting to develop ethics statements based on the values in the Ten Commandments might approve the following:

1. God and family first, then the job.
2. Language used will be without derogatory or swearing words.
3. Employees are allowed one day per week for religious services and the office will not be open on Sunday.
4. Employees will have two weeks of paid family leave per year.
5. Anyone convicted of a crime will be immediately dismissed from employment.
6. Everyone involved with the organization will always be expected to be truthful.
7. Extra marital affairs can be cause for immediate dismissal.
8. Salaries and wages will be based on the average amounts paid for similar jobs within the community.

Chapter Six
Step #3: Develop a Donor Bill of Rights

Your nonprofit depends on the voluntary contributions of tangible and intangible gifts in order to fulfill the vision and mission and to build safe and healthy communities. Donors who make such contributions, whether corporations or individuals, are known as philanthropists.

To ensure donors are respected and can trust your nonprofit will use their donation to meet the mission, rather than for self-interests, develop a Donor Bill of Rights. The process of putting this type of document together can be extremely helpful as a backdrop for gift acceptance policies. That is because even if a controversial individual or organization wants to contribute, how you treat the potential and controversial donor can have long-term ramifications.

If the philanthropist is offended by the way you refuse their gift, you can be sure everyone within their circle will hear about it. And that is not good for building a positive brand identity for your nonprofit.

Things to consider when putting together your bill of rights include:

- No coercion – No one involved with the organization will put pressure on any individual or company to contribute
- Professional relationships – All relationships with donors will be strictly professional and

be based on representing the nonprofit and its vision and mission

- Transparency – Every donor has the right to receive copies of the most recent financial statements
- Leadership – Donors will know who the key staff and members of the board of directors are and will expect them to provide prudent judgement in all decision making
- Guarantee – Donors can expect contributed funds will be used for the purposes stated
- Information – The nonprofit will provide timely information on the vision, mission, outcomes measurements, and programs
- Core mission support[3] – The donor will receive accurate information on the costs for core mission support, such as administrative and fundraising costs
- Confidentiality – Donor information will be protected and kept confidential, to the extent required by law, unless approved in writing for use in media promotions or leadership giving programs. Upon request the organization will delete the donor's name from mailing lists
- Solicitation – Donors will be informed if the individual requesting the donation is an employee of the organization, a volunteer or a hired solicitor

---

[3] ©2017, *Nonprofit Toolkit #5: Developing and Marketing a Story-telling Budget,"* Marilyn L. Donnellan, *www.amazon.com/author/mldonnellan*

- Truth – Donor questions will be answered promptly, truthfully and without withholding important information.
- Conflict of Interest – No one involved with the organization will accept goods or services in exchange for acceptance of a contribution on behalf of the nonprofit.

Addendum D includes examples of a couple of different forms for agreements between donors and your nonprofit. The first example is a generic, simple form which can be used for acceptance or denial of all types of gifts. The second is written from a legal perspective to protect the donor who is giving food donations to a food bank, and to protect the nonprofit. This type of form should be considered for the acceptance of any tangible gift.

For examples of a Donor Bill of Rights see Addendum A, or contact the Association of Fundraising Professionals (https://afpglobal.org/), the Association for Healthcare Philanthropy (www.ahp.org), the Council for Advancement and Support of Education (www.case.org), or the Giving Institute (www.givingusa.org) .

Chapter Seven
Step #4: Develop Gift Acceptance Policies

Components of your gift acceptance policies (GAP) will vary, depending on the vision and mission of your organization. Nonprofits focused on controversial issues, like abortion, environmental issues, politicians, or political parties will be more apt to need stringent policies. That is because public scrutiny of controversial individuals or groups who may have contributed can have negative ramifications.

During the 2016 presidential campaign, the Republican Party attempted to show contributions to the Clinton Foundations by Russia and Saudi Arabia may have influenced Secretary of State Hilary Clinton's decision making while she was in office. Similar accusations were made against candidate Donald Trump and his foundation before and after the election. Apparently, neither presidential candidate had gift acceptance policies in place, and they were forced to deal with the fallout when unacceptable or controversial gifts were received. Greed won out over good sense, apparently.

Purpose of Policies

At the beginning of your GAP, state the purposes: "To clarify for donors and XYZ nonprofit what types of gifts will be accepted, from whom, and how all donors will be treated."

Forms

It is a good idea to offer forms (Addendum D) to potential donors of both tangible items and cash. These completed forms not only provide you with needed information for your donor database, but also for the possible review by the auditor and/or IRS. Include on each form the following acceptance statement:

"We will gladly accept all cash, planned gifts (such as charitable remainder trusts, life insurance and wills) and tangible items as contributions, with the exceptions listed in our Gift Acceptance Policies. We reserve the right to consult legal counsel or to refuse any tangible or cash gift which does not fit with our vision, mission or policies, or which we are unable to process."

Types of Gifts Accepted and Not Accepted

In this section, outline the types of gifts you will and will not accept. I have listed examples of specific items with questions after each as to why they might be unacceptable.

Unacceptable Gifts:
1. Tangible items which the nonprofit is not equipped to receive include the following examples:
   - Animals: How will you care for them and dispose of them? Will you need to pay Unrelated Business Income (UBI) tax on the sale?
   - Real estate: Are you qualified to know if the property is infested with snakes or

vermin, or dilapidated and will need to be torn down? How will you know fair-market value? Will you need to pay UBI tax? Who will handle the legal and property management issues before you sell it? Is it located in an area which will make it difficult to use or sell? If it has a sinkhole or is a swampy area, is it even saleable? Are there liens on the property?

- Estate administration: If your nonprofit is named in a will as the estate administrator, you may think you do not have a choice but to accept the responsibility. Not true. Is there anyone on staff qualified to dispose of someone's estate? Consult with your attorney before accepting this type of gift.

- Lottery winnings: Did the donor pay taxes on it? Are there any strings attached to the donation? Is anyone on staff qualified to handle large donations? Will you invest the money or use it immediately? If you invest, who is qualified to determine how it will be invested? When and how will you use the funds? How will the funds build the capacity and sustainability of your nonprofit?

- Stock: Is it a good stock or not? How do you know? Should you keep it or sell it? When? Does the type of stock fit with your missions? Are there restrictions related to buy and sell requirements?

- Automobiles or other motorized vehicles: Will you pay UBI tax when you sell it? Can you use it for transportation or for the mission? What about insurance and license costs? What kind of shape is it in? Will it cost more to get it and keep it running than it is worth? Where will you keep it?

- Annuities: Unless you have a financial advisor equipped to evaluate and handle annuities, avoid them. There can be legal issues you will need to address, too.

- Life Insurance: Be careful about receiving life insurance since there are a lot of legal issues. Be sure you have your own insurance agent or attorney evaluate the potential gift. Will there be any payout to the owner? When and for how much? Can the policy be converted to cash? What is the amount you will receive? Will there be UBI tax?

- Other: Any item with patent or intellectual property requirements should be avoided.

2. Cash or tangible items from controversial organizations or individuals
    - Organizations or individuals whose mission, vision, ethics, or values do not match the nonprofit's
    - Organizations or individuals with a conflict of interest (e.g. a company who

which placed a bid to fix your facility's leaking roof makes a significant contribution prior to the board deciding whom to hire.)

- Any organization or individual who is or has been the subject of an IRS or criminal, investigation

3. Conflict of interest: Any tangible item or cash which could be perceived as a conflict of interest. Check with your attorney if there is any hint of conflict of interest related to staff, the nonprofit, or a board member.

Other policies to consider are:

A. Related use rules (see Chapter Two),
B. Valuation requirements,
C. Pre-arranged sale issues.
D. How donations forms should be completed, by whom, and the length of time you need before notifying the donor of the denial or acceptance.
E. Confidentiality statements for all donations; donation accepted or not
F. A statement indicating the nonprofit's right to consult with legal counsel and possible circumstances
G. A suggestion for the donor to consult their appropriate financial or legal advisor prior to making any contribution.
H. Donor conflicts of interest or circumstances when the donor should seek professional advice prior to making a gift

I. Identify types of acceptable restrictions on donations
J. Identify individuals who have the right to accept or deny donations; if a committee is used, identify it.
K. Type and form of gift—identify each type of gift and acceptable forms for each kind
L. Include reporting requirements, such as who, when, and how records of the gifts are made and who writes and sends acknowledgement of gifts; and if there are any IRS or legal forms required for certain types of gifts
M. A regular review (annually) of GA Policies and by whom should be stated as a policy.

Now you have drafted the GAP, consider how they will be approved and disseminated.

Chapter Eight
Step #5: Approve and Disseminate Policies

When you have completed drafting all the policies and forms, give them to an attorney familiar with wills, estates, and nonprofits. Their review will help you to avoid legal entanglements. However, most attorneys will try to rewrite the policies in legal terms, which is not necessary. Ask them only to verify the policies are legal and do not violate any laws. Your policies need to be readable and understandable, so avoid legalese.

Once the draft is approved by your attorney, take them back to the committee which drafted them for approval. The chair of the committee (preferable a board member) will take the Giving Acceptance Policies to the board of directors for final approval.

As part of the committee duties, recommendations can be made to you, the ED, on procedures for implementation of the policies. The format suggested in Addendum C will help. Remember: policies are approved by the board and procedures are approved and implemented by the ED.

Dissemination of the policies might include the following:
- Develop the Donor Bill of Rights into a brochure or one-page document which can be put on your website and given to all donors and potential donors

- The approved GAP manual will be made available on your website
- Train staff on all aspects of the policies, especially the resource development or fundraising staff.
- Marketing staff can determine how best to promote the GAP, which might include a media article, on your Facebook and LinkedIn pages, etc.

Finally, once the policies are disseminated and used to accept or deny gifts, be alert for any missing policies, or policies needing clarification. You would take draft revisions to the appointed committee for review and approval before taking them to the board of directors.

The designated committee should review the policies at least every other year to see if there are any other changes needed.

Chapter Ten
In Conclusion

If you follow the steps and examples included, you will be able to develop a flexible but specific set of Gift Acceptance Policies which will help you avoid getting caught between your nonprofit's mission, ethics and values, and a controversial donor or donation.

Always begin the development of any policies by understanding and listing their purposes. Define the terms and guidelines you will be using to avoid conflict and miscommunication.

Once you have done these things, you are ready to draft your policies. I have found it very helpful to put together a rough table of contents first, kind of like building a foundation for the policies.

Secondly, clearly define the philosophies behind your policies: Ethics, values, vision, mission, etc. Then you are ready to put together your Donor Bill of Rights. When you think about their rights, you will be more apt to determine the right policies for gift acceptance or denial.

Now you are ready to put draft policies together for approval. Be flexible and include mechanisms for a regular review of the policies to handle unexpected and complicated donations.

Addendum A: Donor Bill of Rights

The Donor Bill of Rights

Donations to XYZ (nonprofit) are based on the following rights of all donors, based on our vision and mission

Vision: All children safe from abuse
Mission: To educate, advocate and support victims of child abuse and their families

I. No coercion – No one involved with XYZ (nonprofit) will pressure any individual or company to contribute.

II. Professional relationships – All relationships with donors will be strictly professional and be based on representing XYZ and its vision and mission.

III. Transparency – Every donor has the right to receive copies of the most recent financial statements.

IV. Leadership – Donors will know who the key staff and members of the board of directors are and will expect them to provide prudent judgement in all decision making.

V. Guarantee – Donors can expect any contributions will be used for the purposes stated.

VI. Information – XYZ will provide the donor with timely information on the vision, mission, outcomes measurements, and programs.

V.   Core mission support[4] – The donor will receive accurate information on the costs for core mission support, such as administrative and fundraising costs.

VI.   Confidentiality – Every donor's personal information will be protected and kept confidential, to the extent required by law, unless approved in writing for use in media promotions or leadership giving programs. Should there be any data breaches (i.e. hacking), the donor will be immediately notified.

VII.   Removal of Data - Upon request XYZ will delete the donor's name from mailing lists

VIII.   Solicitation – Donors will be informed if the individual requesting donations is an employee of the organization, a volunteer, or a hired solicitor

IX.   Truth – Donor questions will be answered promptly, truthfully and without withholding of important information.

X.   Conflict of Interest – No one involved with XYZ will accept goods or services in exchange for XYZ's acceptance of a contribution.

XI. Tax Advice – The donor has the right, and is encouraged, to get advice on any donations from their tax advisor and/or financial advisor

---

[4] ©2017, *Nonprofit Toolkit #5: Developing and Marketing a Story-telling Budget," Marilyn L. Donnellan, www.amazon.com/author/mldonnellan*

Addendum B – Sample Gift Acceptance Policies

Sample #1: *Table of Contents for GAP for San Francisco Conservatory of Music,* *https://sfcm.edu/*

Introduction

Adapted from Nonprofit Risk Management Center
www.nonprofitrisk.org

Sample #2: Simple GA Policies

1. (Name of nonprofit) solicits and accepts gifts consistent with its mission and which support its core programs, as well as special projects.

2.   Donations and other forms of support will generally   be   accepted   from   individuals, partnerships, corporations, foundations, government agencies, or other entities, subject to the following limitations:

   a) Proof of ownership
   b) Must be delivered to the nonprofit
   c) Tangible items must be new or nearly new
   d) No animals

3.   Gifts of real property, personal property or securities may only be accepted upon approval of (name the appropriate review body, such as the gift acceptance   committee,   resource   development committee or the finance committee)

Sample #3: More Detailed GA Policies

We will gladly accept all cash, planned gifts (such as charitable remainder trusts, life insurance and wills) and tangible items as contributions, with the exceptions listed in our Gift Acceptance Policies. We reserve the right to consult legal counsel or to refuse any tangible or cash gift which does not fit with our vision, mission or policies, or which we are unable to process.

Whereas XYZ (nonprofit's name) actively solicits gifts and grants to further the vision, mission, ethics and values of the organization, and

Whereas there is the potential for controversy if certain gifts are accepted, the organization has adopted the following Gift Acceptance Policies.

When considering whether to solicit or accept gifts, the organization will avoid coercion and consider the following factors:

- Legal Counsel – XYZ will seek legal counsel if they believe it is necessary
- Values – whether the acceptance of the gift compromises any of the core values of XYZ
- Compatibility – whether there is compatibility between the intent of the donor and XYZ's use of the gift
- Public relationships – whether acceptance of the gift damages the reputation of XYZ
- Primary benefit – whether the primary benefit is to XYZ, versus the donor
- Consistency – is acceptance of the gift consistent with prior practice?
- Form of gift – is the gift offered in a form XYZ can use without incurring substantial expense or difficulty?
- Effect on future giving – will the gift encourage or discourage future gifts?

All decisions to solicit and/or accept potentially controversial gifts will be made by the Resource Development (RD) Committee of the board in consultation with the executive director (ED). The need for final approval of the board of directors will be determined by the ED. The primary consideration will be the impact of the gift on XYZ.

XYZ will seek the advice of legal counsel in matters relating to acceptance of gifts when appropriate. Review of counsel is recommended for:

- Gifts of securities subject to restrictions or buy-sell agreements
- Documents naming XYZ as trustee, executor, or requiring XYZ to act in any fiduciary capacity
- Gifts requiring XYZ to assume financial or other obligations
- Transactions with potential conflict of interest
- Gifts of property which may be subject to environmental or other regulatory restrictions.

XYZ will not accept gifts which:

- Would result in violation of its corporate charter, vision, mission, ethics or values
- Would result in losing its status as an IRS 501(c)3 nonprofit organization
- Are too difficult or too expensive to administer in relation to their value
- Would result in any unacceptable consequences for XYZ's mission
- Or, for purposes outside XYZ's mission. Decisions on the restrictive nature of a gift, and its acceptance or refusal, shall be made by the RD Committee, in consultation with the executive director

Gifts generally accepted without review by the executive committee include:

- <u>Cash</u> – Cash gifts are acceptable in any form, including by check, money order, credit card, or on-line. Donors wishing to make a gift by credit card must provide the card type (Visa, Discover, MasterCard, American Express), card number, expiration date, security code, and the name of the card holder as it appears on the credit card.
- <u>Marketable Securities</u> – Securities may be transferred electronically to an account maintained at one or more brokerage firms or delivered physically with the transferor's endorsement or signed stock power (with appropriate signature guarantees) attached. All marketable securities will be sold promptly upon receipt unless otherwise directed by XYZ Finance Committee. In some cases, marketable securities may be restricted by applicable securities laws or the terms of the proposed gift; in such instances, the decision whether to accept the restricted securities shall be made by the RD Committee.
- <u>Planned Gifts,</u> such as: Charitable Remainder Trusts, Charitable Lead Trusts, Bequests and Beneficiary Designations under Revocable Trusts, Life Insurance Policies, Commercial Annuities (under certain circumstances) and Retirement Plans. Donors are encouraged to make such planned gifts or bequests to XYZ through their specific instruments or policies.

Gifts Accepted Subject to Prior Review – Certain forms of gifts or donated properties may be subject to review prior to acceptance. Examples of gifts subject to prior review include, but are not limited to:

- Tangible Personal Property – The RD Committee shall review and determine whether to accept any gifts of tangible personal property with the following considerations:
  1. Does the property further XYZ's mission?
  2. Is the property marketable?
  3. Are there any unacceptable restrictions imposed on the property?
  4. Are there any carrying costs for the property for which XYZ may be responsible?
  5. Is the title/provenance of the property clear?
- Life Insurance – XYZ will accept gifts of life insurance where named as both beneficiary and irrevocable owner of the policy. The donor must agree to pay, before due, any future premium payments owing on the policy.
- Real Estate – All gifts of real estate are subject to review by the RD Committee. Prior to acceptance of any gift of real estate, XYZ shall require an initial environmental review and inspection by qualified firms. In the event any of the initial reviews reveal potential problems, XYZ may retain a

qualified firm to conduct a more thorough audit. Criteria for acceptance of gifts of real estate include:

1. Is the property useful for the purposes and mission of XYZ?

2. Is the property readily marketable?

3. Are there covenants, conditions, restrictions, reservations, easements, encumbrances, liens, or other limitations associated with the property?

4. Are there carrying costs (including insurance, property taxes, mortgages, notes, or the like) or maintenance expenses associated with the property?

5. Does the environmental review, inspection or audit reflect that the property is damaged or otherwise requires remediation?

Steps for Accepting or Denying a Donation

1. Donor will complete a donation form and receive a copy of the Gift Acceptance Policies

2. Donation reviewed by the ED to determine if it meets donation policies or needs to be reviewed by RD Committee

3. If approved, the donor will be notified within 30 days or less by a letter of thanks and acknowledgement, and a copy of the donation form signed by the ED.

4. Copies of the approved donation form will be given to the RD Committee and accounting departments for entry into the database and accounting system.

5. If denied and the donation or donor is controversial, the RD Committee will have the decision reviewed by legal counsel.

6. If denied, the donor will be notified within 30 days or less by a letter, expressing thanks for considering XYZ, and the reasons for the denial.

7. Any negative responses or publicity as a result of the denial will be handled by the ED and adhere to XYZ's crisis communication policies.

Addendum C: Sample Gift Acceptance Manual Format

The table format makes it easy to keep track of policies and procedures. If computerized, searches can be made by topic and categories can be hyperlinked. This same format works for any policy manual you develop. By adding a "cost" column you are more apt to be alert for any impact the policies or procedures have on the annual budget.

Policy	Date Approved by Board	Procedures	Date Approved by ED	Cost
The RD Committee will develop donation acceptance and denial policies for board approval	8/15/2019	1. Donor will complete a donation form and receive a copy of the Gift Acceptance policies 2. The ED will review controversial donations before sending to RD Committee	8/20/2019	Print Brochures and post on website $500

Addendum D: Sample Gift Acceptance Forms

<u>Simple Donation Form</u>

Organization name
Address
Mission statement
Donor Information

Business	Name
Street Address	Email
City, State, Zip	Phone
Website	Alternate Phone

Donation Description

	Date
Check one: ___Cash ___ Check ___Item ___Service ___Other _____Credit card information Signature of donor:_____	
Amount and description Designated to:	
___Donation Accepted ___Initials ___Donation Denied _____Initials	Date

____ "I (donor) do NOT want my donation information made public or used in media releases."
____ "I (donor) DO want my donation information made public or used in media releases."
XYZ Contact
Title, Phone, Website, Email

For Office Use Only:
Indicate date completed
1. Acknowledgement and "thank-you" to donor _____
2. Donor data and donation entered into accounting _____
3. Donor data given to RD staff _____
4. Donor data added to Leadership Giving data (where appropriate) _____

Sample Food Donation Agreement

This Agreement is dated _____, between the ("Donor"), _____, and XYZ nonprofit ("Recipient").

WHEREAS, in connection with its production activities, Donor has and will have leftover foodstuffs and other consumables ("Goods"), Donor wishes to donate such Goods to Recipient, pursuant to the terms of this Agreement.

1. Donation: Free Distribution

Donor hereby donates the Goods to Recipient. Recipient represents and warrants, a) the Goods will be distributed for free to Recipient's clients, b) Recipient is a 501(c)3, tax-exempt, tax deductible nonprofit organized for religious, charitable, or educational purposes and does not provide net earnings to, or operate in any other manner that inures to the benefit of any officer, employee, stakeholder of Recipient, c) Recipient is knowledgeable of the standards to properly recondition donated food or grocery products, and d) Recipient is not providing anything of monetary value to Donor in consideration of the Goods.

2. Inspection

Recipient acknowledges inspection of each donation of Goods, and satisfaction with their condition.

3. Release

Recipient, for itself and its successors, assigns, agents, employees, and representatives, hereby releases and discharges the Donor and each of their former, current and future directors, officers, shareholders, predecessors, successors, assigns, affiliates, board members, agents, insurance carriers, attorneys, servants, employees (including without limitation any catering company engaged for the preparation and delivery of the Goods) from each and every claim, cause of action, damages (including consequential damages) and demands, loss and expense, including but not limited to attorney's fees and costs, that it has or might have, in any way arising out of or in connection with this Agreement or the Goods, except to the extent that any such liability cannot be released or waived under applicable Federal, state or local law. The foregoing shall, to the fullest extent of applicable law, be in addition to, and not in replacement or substitution of, any legal protections offered by any "Good Samaritan" or other similar laws in any jurisdiction.

4. Warranty Disclaimer

Donor hereby expressly disclaims all warranties, written or oral, statutory, express or implied, including any warranty of wholesomeness, merchantability, condition, quality, fitness for use, or suitability of the Goods in any respect whatsoever, including any warranty regarding the absence of any defects therein, whether latent or patent; it being understood and agreed that the Goods are being donated in their current condition as of the date hereof. In connections with Donor's donation of the Goods, Donor shall in no event be liable for any claim whatsoever by or through Recipient, or any third party, for any issue or problem with the Goods, whether such claim is based in any form of warranty, contract, tort (including negligence), strict liability or otherwise and whether for direct, incidental, consequential, exemplary or other damages, except to the extent that any such liability cannot be released or waived under applicable Federal, state or local law. Donor neither assumes nor authorize any person to assume on their behalf any liability in connection with the use or reuse of the Goods.

XYZ signature: _____

Donor signature: _____

About the Author

 **Marilyn L. Donnellan, MS,** has more than 40 years' experience as a nonprofit CEO and consultant. The nonprofits where she served ranged in size from a single staff organization with a budget of $150,000 to a $6 million nonprofit with 300 staff. Her knowledge of all issues related to nonprofit management is the basis for her more than 60 books, toolkits, and webinars in use in more than a dozen countries. She has also written several self-help books and fiction novels. Her team of Authorized Dealers promote and use her material. She has a bachelor's degree in Human Resources Management and a master's degree in Administration

Other Books by M. L. Donnellan, MS
www.amazon.com/author/mldonnellan

- *The Complete Guide to Church Management* (English),
- The *Nonprofit Management Simplified* series on*: Internal Operations, Board and Volunteer Development,* and *Programs and Fundraising*
- *The Nonprofit Toolkits*

Connect with the Author
mldonnellanauthor@gmail.com
www.mldonnellan.com